Cry of the People and Other Poems

CRY OF THE PEOPLE
AND
OTHER POEMS

BY

KIM CHI HA

AUTUMN PRESS

The translations of the poems in this collection are the work of an international group of Kim Chi Ha's friends and associates and the editorial staff of Autumn Press. Not poets themselves, the translators felt that getting the message of these poems into print at this time was of the utmost importance. Much of the purely poetic character of the Korean-language originals has been lost in the process, for which the translators take full responsibility. Several of the shorter poems and portions of *Groundless Rumors* and *Five Bandits* have appeared in RONIN Magazine, and the publishers would like to thank the editors of RONIN for permission to reprint them here.

Published by Autumn Press, Inc.,
with editorial offices at
2113 Isshiki, Hayama, Kanagawa-ken, Japan

ISBN 0–914398–03–2

PRINTED IN JAPAN

You know, we are two-bit actors
And the spectators had better be cold-blooded types.
We have to make them laugh as we die, torn apart,
Vomiting blood.
Dying is wonderful, you know,
    because it happens only once.

(*From* Rope Walker, *1971*)

CONTENTS

INTRODUCTION

KIM CHI HA's fiery verses are rooted in centuries of Korean experience. Little known or understood in the West, the Korean people have had a long and tragic history. Among present-day nations, Korea was one of the first to emerge as a united country, its boundaries and ethnic composition remaining today what they were over a thousand years ago, when the rugged mountainous kingdom first came to be known as Koryo, or "high and beautiful." Since that time it has only been in brief transitional periods that Korea has ever been divided—as it is today along the 38th parallel.

Coming early in its history under Chinese influence, Korean government was organized along Chinese lines and became a complex of ministries put into the service of three successive imperial dynasties, which ruled from the year 668 A.D. to the present century. Korean society came to consist of a small, nonproductive landowner-official class ruling over a mass of commoners and peasants, whose taxes and *corvée* labor supported the government and enriched the hereditary aristocracy. Large aristocratic families competed ruthlessly for the power and wealth concentrated in the great homes and palaces of Seoul, the nation's capital since 1394, while the rural peasantry struggled for survival in wretched poverty. Particularly during the final centuries of the Yi dynasty (1392–1910), exploitation by landlords, nepotism, corruption among officials, despotism, famine and banditry became the Korean way of life.

Japanese annexation of Korea in 1910 brought the Yi dynasty to an end. Long interested in the region for economic reasons, as well as for its possible role as a "land-bridge" to Asia, the Japanese governed their new colony tyrannically. Police controls, backed by the army, were used to suppress all expressions of a modern nationalism that had grown up during the closing decades of the previous century. All political activities were prohibited and all publications were strictly monitored, as the Japanese tightened their grip on what they considered to be an inferior people. By the 1930s, the Korean language was banned and Koreans were compelled to take Japanese surnames, while Japanese economic exploitation led to the continual deterioration of the Korean living standard. As the Japanese extended their hegemony over the Asian mainland, Korea became deeply submerged in the Japanese empire.

Japanese annexation gave rise to patriotic resistance, which focused in the March First movement of 1919. Influenced by Woodrow Wilson's advocacy of the right of all peoples to self-determination, the March First movement took the form of a nationwide non-violent demonstration of Korean nationalism. The Japanese reacted brutally, jailing 19,000 persons, wounding 2,000, and killing 7,000 in the twelve months that followed. World opinion did not then come to Korea's aid, but non-violence has remained at the core of Korean resistance ever since.

One of the most important stimulants to Korean nationalism after the opening of the country to Western contacts in 1882 were Christian missions: Catholic, Presbyterian and Methodist. Most of the Protestant missionaries were American, and the schools, colleges and universities they set up nourished Korean patriotism and molded it in accordance with Christian and liberal values. University students thus took an active role in the March First movement, and in all subsequent actions aimed at establishing liberal democracy in modern Korea. The educational institutions set up under Christian influences became the fountainhead of modern Korean democratic sentiment and ideals.

After the collapse of the Japanese empire in 1945, after suffering thirty-six years of harsh colonial rule and after fighting on the side of the Allies, Korea was again victimized by her geographic location and historical circumstances. Chinese, Russian and American interests in the region clashed. Roosevelt and Stalin agreed at Yalta to divide Korea temporarily along the 38th parallel while enforcing the surrender of Japanese forces. The joint U.S.-U.S.S.R. commission to speed unification of north and south, however, soon feel prey to the tensions of the cold war that divided the former allies. In 1947, the United States brought the dispute before the United

11

Nations, and in May 1948 a South Korean National Assembly was chosen in general elections held under U.N. auspices. A democratic constitution was adopted in the following July, and American-educated Synghman Rhee became the first president of the Republic of South Korea, proclaimed on August 10, 1948. Meanwhile, as Soviet forces entered North Korea, Communist-trained Koreans set up a Soviet-style state in the north under the leadership of Kim Il Sung, sending a million anti-communist North Koreans—mostly Christians—escaping to the South.

On June 25, 1950, North Korean military forces attacked across the border into South Korea, embroiling America, China and Russia, as well as Britain and other member nations of the U.N., in a tragic war which resulted in 142,000 American and over 1.5 million Korean and Chinese casualties. An armistice was signed in Panmunjon on July 27, 1953, which is still in effect, while the country remains divided. Ironically, U.N. procurements for this war sped Japanese recovery from its wartime devastation.

In the years since the Korean war, the United States has poured some $35 billion in aid into South Korea to hasten its rehabilitation and strengthen it as a bulwark against communism in Asia. But Synghman Rhee's autocratic rule, police represssion, official corruption and rigged elections sparked student demonstrations in Seoul in April 1960, forcing Rhee to resign and go into exile. A civilian government headed by Prime Minister John M. Chang and President Yun Po Sun was established in June, but was overthrown less than a year later by a *coup d'état* led by Major General Chung Hee Park, who formed a military regime. Pressures emanating from both within and without South Korea forced Park to hold elections in October 1963, in which he was chosen to head a civilian government.

After his election, Park began a drive to suppress the opposition, the press and his political opponents, creating the dreaded Korean Central Intelligence Agency (KCIA) to serve as an arm of authoritarian control over the Korean people. Park was "re-elected" in 1967, and again in 1971 after forcing a constitutional amendment through the Assembly permitting him to serve more than two terms. In October 1972, under martial law declared on the pretext of an alleged threat of internal subversion and invasion by the North, Park promulgated a revised (*Yushin*) constitution which denied such basic human rights as the freedoms of speech, press and assembly. In addition, it gave Park personal control over the appointment of judges to the judicial branch, as well as the power to dissolve the National Assembly at will. In effect, the *Yushin* Constitution established one-man rule and virtually deprived the Korean people of the right to choose their own government.

After months of growing student and intellectual protests calling for reversion to the former constitution, Park issued four "emergency decrees" between January and April 1974. The first two, issued on January 8 and carrying a maximum penalty of 15 years imprisonment, banned all forms of objection to the new constitution and set up special courts-martial to try accused violators. A third decree issued on January 14 gave Park extraordinary powers to steer the nation through economic difficulties allegedly arising from the worldwide oil crisis. Finally, on April 3, an even harsher decree with a penalty of up to death was issued to crack down on a clandestine student body, the National Federation of Democratic Youth and Students, accused of an attempt to overthrow the Park government and set up a Communist regime in Seoul. It was under this decree that nine people were sentenced to death and twenty others, including dissident poet Kim Chi Ha and student leaders, were given life imprisonment. Also prominent among the convicted were former president Yun Po Sun, who received a suspended three-year sentence, and Roman Catholic Bishop Daniel Tji, sentenced to a 15-year prison term. Although Park rescinded the first and last of these decrees after an August 1974 assasination attempt that resulted in the death of his wife, the former sentences remain valid and court-martial trials already pending will continue.

South Korea's most acclaimed poet and most outspoken critic of Chung Hee Park's authoritarian regime, Kim Chi Ha was born on February 4, 1941, in Mokpo, located in South Korea's southern *Chollo-Do* province. Kim entered Seoul National University's College of Liberal Arts and Sciences in 1959, only to have his studies suffer from various interruptions. He spent parts of 1961 and 1962 "wandering" in the Korean countryside, then, after returning to the university, took part in the 1964 student movement against talks being conducted for the normalization of relations between Japan and her former colony. Suspected of leadership and organizational roles in the student demonstrations, Kim was tortured and imprisoned. Nevertheless, after his release he participated in the 1965 movement against the Japan-Korea normalization treaty.

After graduating from the university in 1966 with

a degree in aesthetics, Kim once again took to the road, working at odd jobs and writing. In 1967 he found that his tuberculosis had become chronic, and he was forced to spend the next two years in a sanitorium. Leaving the hospital in 1969, he worked at a movie script, in theater workshops and at other related projects, continuing all the while to write poetry. Kim then made his debut in a poetry magazine and became steadily more involved in his poems. In 1970 he published "Five Bandits" in a popular intellectual literary magazine. Interpreted as condemning various aspects of mis-used power in modern Korea, the poem was well-received and was reprinted by the opposition in its party organ. The newspaper was then confiscated by the KCIA, and the poet, the magazine's publishers, as well as other figures, were all arrested under the Anti-Communist Law. After a lengthy imprisonment and court proceedings, the defendants were freed on bail, with charges still hanging over their heads. Three months after his release from jail, where he was again tortured, the poet's first anthology, *Yellow Earth*, was published.

In April 1972, Kim Chi Ha published "Groundless Rumors," another poem critical of the Establishment, this time in the Catholic magazine *Creation*. The magazine's publisher and American-priest editor were interrogated by the KCIA, and the magazine was allowed to survive only on condition that the editor be removed. The poet, who had been leading a semi-nomadic existence in the Korean countryside in order to avoid further police and KCIA interference, was tracked down, arrested and sent to a sanitorium in Masan. He was forbidden to meet with the foreign press under threats of further penalties being applied to his family and friends, and was eventually charged on May 31 with "having made remarks slandering the incumbent government."

In early May, campaigns were mounted in Japan to secure the poet's release. The international campaign organized for the poet from Tokyo included such luminaries as Jean-Paul Sartre, Simone de Beauvoir, Herbert Marcuse, Costa Gavras, Howard Zinn, Noam Chomsky, Alain Robbe-Grillet, Jean Pouillon, Claude Simon and Louis Malle. In early July, a delegation of Japanese writers managed to deliver a copy of the petition to the Prime Minister's office in Seoul and visited the poet in his Masan sanitorium. Kim Chi Ha was subsequently released on July 18, 1972.

After publication of his "Cry of the People," Kim was arrested again in April 1974, as Park escalated his campaign to silence mounting criticism of his police state. In early July he was convicted of supporting the Federation of Democratic Youth and Students which allegedly organized the student and Christian demonstrations against the Park dictatorship in March and April. He was sentenced to death, and only immense international pressure brought to bear on behalf of Kim and other political prisoners in South Korea forced the Korean government to back down and commute the poet's sentence to life imprisonment.

While Kim languishes in jail, his poetry has become the rallying cry of all of his countrymen who oppose tyranny and oppression. But the 33-year-old poet speaks for the oppressed of mankind everywhere, and his message cries out to all men and women of conscience. His poems are attacks upon the corruption of governmental officialdom, the erosion of human rights, and the suffering of the impoverished people of South Korea and the rest of the world. Although he prefers to think of himself as a comedian, Kim Chi Ha has found the cry of the people reverberating through his pen and, though it may cost him his life, he has surrendered to it. The cry and the poet have become one. Neither will be silenced.

NICOLA GEIGER

September, 1974
Tokyo, Japan

Excerpts from Conversations with Kim Chi Ha (1972)

On South Korean Politics

I'm always feeling pity, deep pity, for the government. But because the reality is one suppressing basic civil rights and basic democracy, I cannot help crying out against the government. Of course I know that this country is very underdeveloped, and that in the cold war climate there is yet a very delicate and difficult problem here. I know. I can understand that deep in my heart. I can also understand how difficult this government's role is. But I think that when one cannot manage power, one must give it up.

On His Friends

You know, I'm not the only one. More than I have done this. One hundred seventy of my friends were tortured in March. But that's not new. They tortured them this year and two years ago and five years ago. It's a part of life for those around me. Sunday is my confirmation day and I must forgive them (the government and KCIA), but I can't. Even after I'm dead I'll not be able to forgive them. I want to, but I can't.

On Kim Chi Ha

My problem is nothing. I'm not a Solzhenitsyn, you know. I'm Kim Chi Ha. Not a tragic figure. A comic, like these bad teeth of mine. I feel happy in any situation. But the chance to write freely, that's what I hope for now. The chance to write freely.

Cry of the People and Other Poems

The Yellow Dust Road

Following the vivid blood, blood on the yellow
    road,
I am going, Father, where you died.
Now it's pitch dark, only the sun scorches.
Hands are barbed-wired.
The hot sun burns sweat and tears and rice-paddies
Under the bayonets through the summer heat.
I am going, Father, where you died,
Where you died wrapped in a rice-sack
When the trouts were jumping along the *Pujuu*
    brookside,
When the blaze rose from *Opo* Hill every night,
On that day when the sun shone brightly on
    the yellow land,

The muddy land resilient as the gorses that grow
    intrepidly green.

Shall we cry out the call of that day?
Shall we sing the song of that day?

In small *Whadang* village embraced among the
    sparse bamboo-bushes,
Blood surges up in every well, every ten years.
Born in this barren colony,
Slain under the bayonets, my Father,
How could the dew in the bamboo-buds that
    spring
Forget, ever forget the crystal brightness of May?
It was a long and cruel summer,
When even the children were starving,
That sultry summer of blatant tyranny
That knew not of the Heavens
Or the yellow road, eternally our motherland,
Our hope.

Following the muddy beach where the sun burns
    the old wooden boats to dust,
Again through the rice paddies
And over the bleached, whitish furrows.
It's been ten years since the call of that day
That thundered against the ever blue and high
    firmament—
The flesh, the breath, tightened by barbed-wire.
I can hear your voice.

24

I am going now, Father, where you died
When the trouts were jumping along the
    Pujuu brookside,
Where you died
Wrapped in a rice-sack.
Where you died.

Kim Chi Ha's native *Cholla-Do* province has for centuries been a hotbed of revolutionary fervor. *The Yellow Dust Road* commemorates a rising of *Cholla-Do* villagers in protest against the abject circumstances of the early postwar period. *Whadang*'s bamboo bushes were cut and fashioned into staves to be used against the military forces sent to quell the rebellion by the Synghman Rhee government. The fires ignited on *Opo* Hill signalled the start of the uprising, in which one-third of the village's six hundred farmers were massacred alongside *Pujuu* Brook.

The Sea

Brimming
Pooling sea
In the hollow faces,
In the hollow scars left by the whip,
In the shadow of peasants' hollow eyes . . . sea.
In the unopened parched lips,
And unopened prisons . . . sea,
Pooling sea.
Small, silent sea of anger.
Brimming; while waves gather
Candle-light permeates the torn body;
I writhe and struggle:
Oh, oppression!
Sometimes dancing sea, glistening but
Not moonlit, not burning.
Small. Oh, oppression!
Silent sea of anger
Someday suddenly overflowing,
Someday mercilessly surging forth,
Ceaselessly, silently, flowing
In the forearm digging the soil.
In the eyes, lips and breast,
Pools the sea, little by little . . .
The Sea of Storm, not yet risen.

The Road To Seoul

I must go.
Don't cry, I must go
On the burdensome road to Seoul,
Climbing the white and black thirsting hills
To sell my chastity.

Without a promise of when I'll return,
When I'll come back with brightly blooming smiles,
And without the humble promise of untying the
    ribbon
I must go.
However hard and miserable life may be,
How can I ever forget the hills covered with
    castor-bean flowers and the smell of wheat
    growing in the fields surrounding the village
    where I was born.

I'll not forget, but cherish them deeply in my heart.
I might come back in tearful dreams;
I might return with starlight in the night.

I must go.
Don't cry, I must go
On the burdensome road to Seoul,
Climbing the thirsty hills which make even the
        sky weary,
To sell my chastity.

Korea's harsh and barren hillsides have come to represent
the peasants' struggle for survival. The castor bean flower,
which grows profusely throughout the Korean countryside,
symbolizes the peasants' lowly estate and relative power-
lessness. "Untying the ribbon" is a traditional Korean symbol
of the marriage vows.

April Blood

Burn!
Crazed by the fragrance
From the breast of the coarse yellow earth,
Suffocating fragrance,
Fragrance brightly illuminating darkness.
Burn in the chaotic darkness,
Crazed by bright, lucid existence
In the decaying flesh, in the rotten spirit.
Burn!
In the pitch-black darkness
Of the eyes' rotten pupils.
Crazed by the fragrance,
Crazed by the suffocating scent of the fragrance.
In the chaotic end of darkness,
Flowing blood, burn!
Burn the eternal oppression
Of silence standing aloft in the darkness.
Oh, April blood
Fragrance dispersing brightly even in the darkness;
Crazed by clear bright life.

April Blood commemorates South Korea's student revolution of 1960 that brought on the collapse of the Synghman Rhee regime and the first change of leadership since the Korean Republic's foundation after World War II. Some 500 people, most of them students, were killed during the uprising.

Parting

Farewell, farewell.
Passing the low silvery hills,
Passing the dancing flowers
In the quivering shade of the grove,
Vanishing city
Where my bloody youth was buried,
Farewell.
Winds fluttering restlessly
Among the fallen shacks,
Among the collapsed fences.
Sunrays yelling, tearing apart the yellow earth.
Heavy silence
Suppresses the crying all around,
And in the heart, sadness burns.

In worn-out overalls, in the crumpled body
This long, long lamentation burning.
Unextinguishable lamentation.
Blue flames of grief
Neither oblivion nor death can quench.
Not a day could I sleep without drinking;
Not a day could I live without fighting.
Life was shame; life was scorn; I couldn't even die.
Nowhere on earth to go, setting everything
        on fire.
I cried and cried,
And they trampled and trampled;
The very last handful of youth's pride
Torn into strips.
With the opiate injected
I finally fell asleep.
My eyes became those of gentle sheep.
Head bent,
I bid farewell to my tired shadow.
With eyes raised again
'Tis rather a strange land . . .
Villages, woods, crimson earth, I kiss with tears.
I embrace the naked sufferings of tomorrow's earth
Which I must fight for again, laying down my life.
Nostalgia surges fully into mad and rebellious
        hearts.
The smell of earth deep, deep in my heart.
Friends! Who have struggled fearlessly
In this most barren land, never to be forgotten,
Once again let us embrace,
The bloody bitter days long gone by.

Farewell.
Passing the gleaming yellow dust road beside tall
    poplars,
Passing the quivering shades of the grove.
Vanishing city,
Farewell, farewell.

Parting was written in 1966 after Kim Chi Ha's graduation
from Seoul National University and as he left the capital to
travel through the Korean countryside.

Hunger

Ah, my belly's empty!
Pulling up weeds
I lie down and drink spring water,
Use a rock as my pillow.
I'll eat roots, gulp down dirt and wild flowers,
Bright red poison mushrooms,
Yet still have an empty belly.
I could devour animals by the hundreds,
      thousands—hard ones.
I want to eat pork, put away fat ones.
I'll eat you.
I've been driven mad by long starvation,
Dragging this enormous empty gut along the
      ground.
I will leave the country where there is nothing
      to eat
And go to Seoul,
Picking up food along the way:
Fishbones, sprouts,
Rib-bones leftover by the dogs,
Eggs, houses, streets,
Pieces of iron.
Male and female,
Anything that has grown fat —
I'll even eat human flesh.
Ah, I'm so unbearably hungry
I could eat money.

The Sun

The sun was only as wide as a man's foot.
Not a single person knows of the cyclone
    approaching,
Steadily approaching.
In the fields, however,
The leaves dance to and fro in the wind—
The wind has been known to move mountains.
The waves are not quiet for a moment.
Do you know that the blade has at last corroded?
You would not know though the wind howled by.
The sun was only as wide as a man's foot. Idiot
    sun!
The fire-tempered steel melts in the fire;
The water-reared city falls asleep in the water.

No one knows, now
On the streets, every night,
People let out cries from their nightmares.
Sometimes people go mad! Do you know?
You probably don't know that the blade has
    corroded.
Do you know or don't you?
Was there ever a night when you were not
    whipped?
There was probably never a day when rocks did
    not fly at you.
Never a day, of course!
Like being worn away by water,
Like a boulder being constantly worn away—like
    that!
I say the day will come
The old sword's blade rotted away—while
    weeping —
When it cannot even cut the wind—while weeping
    aloud —
Do you know the rusted blade?
The sun's an idiot. Do you know?
The sun was only as wide as a man's foot. Do
    you know or not?
Damn it!
You could not be expected to know.

No Return

I shall not return having once stepped into this
    place.
If I sleep, it is the sleep which cuts deeply into
    the flesh —
That sleep, that white room, that bottomless
    vertigo.

The sound of high leather boots in the night,
The place where they come and go on the ceiling,
Invisible faces, hands, gestures,
That room where voices and laughter arise —
That white room, that bottomless vertigo.
Opening my eyes
With the pain of a fingernail being pulled out,
Crying, my body being torn apart,
My wizened soul alone remaining.
Can I not depart?
In vain,
Comrades who died in vain,
Fallen into humiliating sleep,
Fallen into sleep in vain.
In the past
Sometimes faintly smiling, sometimes crying out—
Those wonderful friends.
Ah, I shall not return, not return.

Blue Suit

Wish I were a bird,
Water, or else wind.

Imprisoning the thin naked body, this suit of
Blue! Wish the blue were the sea.
Could the sea gleam even in my brief dream.

Sticking in my heart, bleeding painfully,
And then clotting into the square scarlet mark . . .
But for it —
But for it
I might not refuse death;
Even a destiny scattered in ashes would not matter.

In eyes anxiously awaiting dawn
On such a dark night,
In the clear tears overflowing,
Could the crystal morning-glory dazzle just once,
Could the sun's rays shine.

Vivid blue sky opening
Through the dark clouds in nightly dreams . . .
Could I stand in spilling sunrays a moment.
Willingly would I die imprisoned in the blue suit;
Were it real,
Were it now,
For ever and ever
Willingly would I die.

The inmates of South Korea's prisons wear blue uniforms. Prisoners accused or convicted of violations of the Anti-Communist Law wear in addition a red-plastic badge about three centimeters square pinned over the left breast.

I want to write a poem with candid and bold words and without any hesitation. It's been a long time since I was last beaten up for writing with unruly pen. My body is itching to be beaten; my mouth is eager to speak, and my hands are dying to write. Since my urge to write is beyond my control, I have made up my mind to write a story concerning strange bandits. I am doing this knowing that it will invite serious punitive measures, including physical pain.

It's the best story you've ever seen with your navel or heard with your anus since the country was formed under Mt. *Paektu*[1] on the third of October long long ago.

Five Bandits

We are now enjoying times of great peace that are unprecedented since *Tan'gun*[2] founded the nation. In such peaceful and prosperous times, could there be poverty or could there be any bandits? Farmers eat so much that they frequently die of ruptured stomachs! People go naked the year round because they are loath to wear silk garmets anymore!

Ko Chae-pong[3] might claim to be a great bandit, but there were greater during the time of Confucius in China. Corruption and irregularities are on the rampage throughout the country; but, then, there were social evils during the golden age in ancient China too. Regardless of one's position, once one has formed the habit of stealing, one is most likely to retain it for the rest of one's life. Five bandits live as neighbors in the heart of Seoul.

Human waste characterizes the scenery in the southern part of Seoul. To the east, *Dong Bing Ko-dong*'s[4] luxurious mansions border the dirty *Han* River. Barren mountains surround the capital on the north like the hairless rear ends of chickens. Spread below the naked mountains are *Songbuk-Tong* and *Suyu-Dong*.[5] Between the north and south, wooden shacks dot the landscape.

Towering high above the decrepit shacks scattered far below like pockmarks, inside the arrogant, jarring, great gates at *Changch'un-Dong* and *Yaksu-Dong*,[6] are five stately floral palaces, glittering, sparkling, shooting up into the sky without restraint, filled day and night with music and the sounds of feasting. These are the dens of the five bandits, who are unsurpassed in craftiness and brutality, with bloated livers the size of *Nam-san*[7] and necks as tough as *Tonggt'Ak*'s[8] umbilical cord, who are called the Tycoon, the Assemblyman, the Government Official, the General, and the Minister.[9]

Although everyone else has five internal organs and six entrails in his abdomen, these fellows, each endowed with a robber's sack as large as the testicles of a huge bull, have five internal organs and seven entrails. They originally learned robbery from the same master, but each of them developed his potential in a different way. Ceaselessly committing robbery day and night, they developed their skills until they were almost magical.

One day, when the five bandits had gathered together, one of them said: "Ten years ago today each of us, swearing on our blood, opened up in business. Since then we have improved our skills daily, and accumulated more and more gold. How about chipping in for a prize of 100,000 Kun[10] of gold to see which one of us has developed the best techniques over these months and years?" Thus they decided to hold a contest under the slogan "Banditry."

The spring sun was warm, the day pleasant, the wind gentle, the clouds floating by. The five bandits, each brandishing a golf club, each determined to win, set out to display their miraculous skills. The first bandit stepped forth, the one called the business tycoon, wearing a custom-made suit tailored of banknotes, a hat made of banknotes, shoes made of banknotes and gloves knitted of banknotes, with a gold watch, gold rings, gold buttons, a gold necktie pin, gold cuff links, a gold buckle, golden teeth, golden nails, golden toe-nails and golden zippers, with a golden watch chain dangling from his wiggling ass.

Watch the tycoon demonstrate his skill!

Roasting the cabinet minister a beautiful brown, and boiling the vice-minister red, sprinkling soy sauce, mustard, hot sauce, and *MSG*, together with red pepper, welsh onions, and garlic on them, he swallowed them up, together with banknotes collected from taxes, funds borrowed from foreign countries, and other privileges and benefits.

Pretty girls he lured, made his mistresses, and kept busy producing babies. A dozen daughters thus made were given as tribute to high officials as midnight snacks. Their tasks were to collect information on the pillow, thereby enabling him to win negotiated contracts, buy land cheaply, and make a fortune once a road was opened. He claimed in his bids a thousand *won*[11] when five *won* were sufficient to do the work, pocketing the difference as well as withholding laborers' wages.

Even *Son O-Kong*[12] would be no match for his subtle techniques of appropriation, his superb skills of flattery.

Now the second bandit steps forth with his cronies from the National Assembly. Here come hunchbacks, alley foxes, angry dogs, and monkeys. Hunched at the waist, their eyes are as narrow and slanted as *Cho Cho*'s.[13] Lumbering, rasping, covering their hairy bodies with the empty oaths of revolution, coughing

42

up mucus, raising their golf clubs high into the sky like flags, thunderously yelling slogans, rolling on viper-colored jagged floors:

Revolution, from old evil to new evil!

Renovation, from illegal profiteering to profiteering illegally!

Modernization, from unfair elections to elections unfair!

Physiocracy, from poor farms to abandoned farms!

Construction, all houses to be built in *Wawoo*[14] style!

Clean up society, follow *Chong In-Suk*![15] Rise up! Rise up! Bank of Korea notes! Korean rice wine! Fists! Ballots spoiled with numerous seals and pockmarks! Owls, weasels, blindmen, ghosts—all put to use in the holy battle of stealing votes!

Son Ja, that old Chinese strategist, declared long ago that soldiers do not reject vice, that Governors are bandits, that a public oath is an empty oath.

You foolish people, get out of the way! You stink!

Let me play golf!

Now the third bandit emerges, looking like a rubber balloon with viperous pointed eyes, his lips firmly closed! Portraying a clean government official, when sweets are offered, he shows that he doesn't like them by shaking his head. Indeed, it must be true. But look at this fellow's other face. He snoops here and smiles there, stout, impudent, sly; his teeth are crooked and black from an over-indulgence in sweets, worn out until they could decay no more.

He sits in a wide chair as deep as the sea, before a desk as high as the sky. Saying "no thank you" with one hand and "thank you" with the other. He cannot do possible things, but he can do impossible things; he has piles of documents on top of his desk and bundles of money under it. He acts like an obedient shaggy dog when flattering superiors, but like a snarling hunting dog to subordinates. He puts public funds into his left pocket and bribes for favors-done into his right pocket. His face, a perpetual mask of innocence, conveys purity—the purity of a white cloud. His all-consuming passion is asking after the well-being of madams of deluxe restaurants.

The fourth bandit steps forth, a big gorilla. He is tall, reaching almost to the heavens. The marching column of soldiers under his command is as long as China's Great Wall. He has white tinted eyes, a tiger's mouth, a wide nose, and a shaggy beard; he must be an animal. His breast is adorned with colorful medals made of gold, silver, white copper, bronze and brass. Black pistols cling to his body.

He sold the sacks of rice meant to feed the soldiers, and filled the sacks with sand. He stole the cows and pigs to be fed the soldiers, and gave a hair to each man. No barracks for the poor enlisted men in a bitterly cold winter; instead, hard labor all day to keep them sweating. Lumber for the construction of barracks was used for building the general's quarters. Spare parts for vehicles, uniforms, anthracite briquettes, monthly allowances, all were stolen. In accordance with military law, soldiers who deserted their units because of hunger and desperation were arrested, beaten and thrown into the brig, and harassed under orders. University students summoned for military service were assigned to the general's quarters as living toys for his wanton wife. While the general enjoyed his cleverly camouflaged life with an unending stream of concubines.

Now the last bandit and his cronies step out: ministers and vice-ministers, who waddle from obesity, sediment seeping from every pore. With shifty mucus-lined eyes, they command the national defense with golf clubs in their left hands, while fondling the tits of their mistresses with their right. And, when they softly write "Increased Production, Increased Export and Construction" on a mistress's tits, the woman murmers "Hee-hee-hee, don't tickle me!" And they jokingly reproach: "You ignorant woman, do national affairs make you laugh?" Let's export even though we starve, let's increase production even though products go unsold. Let's construct a bridge across the Strait of Korea with the bones of those who have starved to death, so we can worship the god of Japan! Like slave-masters of olden times, they drive the people to work harder and longer, with the beating of bursted drums and the sounds of broken trumpets, with one aim in mind: to increase their own wealth.

They buy a Mercedes in addition to their black sedans, but feign humility by riding in a Corona.[16] They make their fortune by cheating the budget and further fatten it by illegal biddings, but chew gum to rid themselves of the smell of corruption. They shout loudly not to deal in foreign goods, while lighting up a Kent. They hastily write decrees to ban foreign goods and are pleased with how nicely the law was written. They deny their dishonesty to an "ignorant" journalist who, hearing of a big scandal, rushes upon the scene. And for an answer they smugly whisper: "What is your golf handicap?"

Even the ghosts who watched the horrifying cunningness displayed in the contest grew alarmed and fled, for fear that they too would get caught and lose their bones.

The ripened pumpkins of September and October waiting to be harvested were rotting in the fields.

From beyond the blue sky a stern voice was heard rolling like thunder, commanding: "Arrest those bandits who disgrace our national honor!" And an answer was heard, saying: "Yes sir. They will be arrested at once."

And now look at the prosecutor general, with his bumpy pig-nose smeared white with wine sediment, his catfish nose slobbering saliva! His whiskers are as wild as those of *Changbi;*[17] his eyes are red with the blood of the dead; a dangling tumor as big as a fist grows on his forehead. With arms stretched out, roaring like a lion, he kicks and punches men around him at random, removing their skin, chaining them in dungeons.

But listen with me to what was happening.

The order coming from the stern voice behind the blue sky was not followed. The bandits were not arrested. Instead the keeper of the law of the land arrested in a different direction. Blowflies[18] in *Chongno* 3rd Street; big flies in *Myong-Dong*; dirty flies in *Yang-Dong*; nasty flies in *Mugyo-Dong* and *Ch'Onggyech'On*; dung flies in *Wangsim-Ni.*[19] All were collected and assembled in one place where they were beaten, struck, kicked, stamped upon, burnt, pinched, bitten, thrown away, flattened, crushed, punctured, twisted, broken, knifed, bayonetted; infringed upon and bent like the willow branches along the banks of the *Nodul* River.[20]

With six-angled clubs, three-angled iron bars, hooks, long and short swords, large and small swords, large and small knives, ropes, handcuffs, sticks, clubs and whistles. At hand were also dog-legged, cow-legged rifles, submachine guns, hand grenades, tear gas bombs, smoke bombs, dung bombs, urine bombs, dirty water bombs, and more of the latest sophisticated weapons.

All neatly arranged.

The prosecutor general roared arrest orders with a voice as loud as a tiger farting. People dragged out from all parts of the country bowed deep and trembled. Peasants from *Cholla-Do* trembled like the others, as if shivering from severe cold. And he began his questioning:

"You are the five bandits, aren't you?"

"No, sir, I am not."

"Then, who are you?"

"I am a snatcher."

"Aah, good. Snatcher, pickpocket, robber, burglar, and swindler. They are the five bandits."

"No, sir, I am not that kind of snatcher."

"What are you then?"

"I am a pimp."

"Aah, good. A pimp is better. Pimp, prostitute, madam, hoodlum, and informer. You're the five bandits, aren't you?"

"No, no, I am not a pimp."

"Then, what are you?"

"I am a peddler."

"Aah, peddler! Much better. Gum peddler, cigarette peddler, sock peddler, candy peddler, and chocolate peddler. They are the real bandits living on imported goods."

"No, no, sir, I am not that kind of peddler."

"Then, what are you?"

"I am a beggar, sir."

"Aah, if you are a beggar, it is even better. Beggar, leper, ragpicker, pauper, thief, all these together are the five delinquent bandits. Shut up, you dog: to the big house with you!"

"No, no, I don't want to go. I am not the five bandits, I am a peasant from *Cholla-Do*. I came to Seoul to earn my livelihood because I couldn't feed myself by farming. The only crime I committed was stealing a small piece of bread because I was hungry last night."

But nobody listens to him. The rope around him is tightened, left and right, up and down, and he twists hopelessly, listening to the squeaking noises. The tortures used are compressing, beating, water torture, fire torture, tanning, branding, hanging upside down, swinging in the air. Soapy water, to which red repper and vinegar are added, is poured on him. But his answer remains the same: "No, sir. No. No sir."[21] That is all he says.

The prosecutor general is at his wits' end. He needs a confession! Unable to wring one out in spite of

49

infamous tortures, he decides to persuade the victim gently. He suggests that he make a guess as to who the five bandits might be, promising to spare his life. Hearing this, the countryman, more dead than alive, answered: "The five bandits are five animals called Tycoons, Assemblymen, Government Officials, Generals, and Ministers, who are now staging a banditry contest in *Tongbinggo-Dong*."[22]

"Aah those names sound familiar. Are they really animals?"

"Yes, they are very ferocious brutes!"

"I am glad to hear that, my boy! You should have told me before." The prosecutor general, overjoyed, slapped his knees so hard that he cracked one of the bones.

"Hey, boy! Get up! Take the lead! Let's find them and hack them to pieces. I will be a success! I will be famous!"

The young peasant in the lead, the prosecutor general sets out on his mission with dignity and determination, his eyes shining brightly like those of a tiger tensing for the kill. Shouting continuously: "All of you, stand aside! Out of my way! I am going to arrest the bandits!" he marches on:

Tarum tarum tarum-tum-tum, tarum tarum tarum-tum-tum, tarum tarum tarum-tum-tum.

Leaping over *Nam-San*, he overlooks *Tongbinggo-Dong*. The large crowds who had followed him are clapping their hands. To them it seems that General *Yi Wan*[23] has been reborn. The prosecutor general rushes into the battlefield roaring: "Bandits, listen! You nasty beasts who live by sucking the people's blood.

"Your traitorous acts have defamed our national honor!
"People's complaints are heard everywhere!
"By the order of the King, you are under arrest."

The bandits stared at him without blinking an eye. Remember they were animals in appearance, luxurious, colorful animals.

The prosecutor general couldn't believe his eyes. He wasn't sure whether he was dreaming or awake. A paradise before his eyes! The clear blue swimming pool full of naked fairies. In the garden, trees and foreign dogs worth a million *won,* large and small rocks, stone lamps and Buddha statues worth ten million *won,* carp and bream swimming in the pond, and sparrows and quail sitting in cages worth a hundred million *won.* The doors were automatic, the walls were automatic, drinking was automatic, cooking was automatic, women were performing automatic wanton acts, and everything was automatic, automatic, automatic. The housemaids were college girls, the accountants were doctors of economics, the gardeners were doctors of forestry, the house managers were doctors of business administration, the tutors were doctors of philosophy, the secretaries were doctors of politics, the beauticians were doctors of aesthetics, doctors, doctors, and more doctors.

For fear that the grass might freeze, a steam heating system had been installed in the lawn and the ponds were temperature-controlled. Heaters were placed in the bird cages so that the birds would not feel cold, and a refrigerator was placed near the dog house so the dog food would not rot. Korean tiles covered the roof of the western-style, marble-walled residence. The columns were Corinthian and the center beam was Ionic. Truly a palace. The glass rooms had double doors. Artificial grass had been put on the stone walls. The second story had a tiled roof garden with folding windows decorated with the old Chinese character for "bandit." The inner and outer gates were built in Persian style, the bath in Turkish style, and the pig styes in pure Japanese style.

A pond and an artificial mountain had been created nearby. Standing on this mountain he peered into the house through the opened door and saw a cabinet decorated with pearls, a chest decorated with the carving of a Chinese phoenix, a larger chest decorated with carvings of dragons, and an enormous chest decorated with the carving of a carnation; a dish decorated with precious stones as large as an athletic field; candlesticks of gold and bronze as high as the ceiling, an electric clock, an electric rice bowl, an electric kettle, an electric bag, glass bottles, woodenware, celadon and white porcelain. A Piccaso was hung upside down, and a Chagal was hung sideways. The picture of an orchid in a golden frame shone brightly. There were about four hundred vertical scrolls on the walls, and numerous other paintings of mountains, lakes, flowers, birds, butterflies, and people were displayed. There were vases, *Tang* Japanese vases, American vases, French vases, Italian vases; a TV set covered with a tiger's skin, a Sony tape recorder encased in a decorated chest, a Mitchell camera on the desk, an RCA movie projector beside the desk, and a Parker pen in an amber pen holder. Candle-lit chandeliers and castor-oil lamps dazzled the eyes with their direct and indirect rays.

Look at the women's accessories! Sapphire hairpins decorated with white precious stones, ornamented shoes, golden broaches, white gold false teeth, amber ear plugs, coral anus plugs, ruby navel plugs, golden buttons, pearl earings, diamond nose rings, violet quartz necklaces, sapphire bracelets, emerald anklets, diamond belts, and Turkish eyeglass frames made of stone.

And yet the five bandits wore brass rings worth a measely three *won* on their pudgy fingers, for didn't they shine like torches in the night!

The prosecutor general turned around, peering through another open door. And what did he see: great quantities of delicious foods piled high on large tables. Cow hair steaks, fried pig snouts, fried goat's whiskers, boiled deer antlers, skewered and roast chicken legs, dried pheasant fin, fried sea bream fin, salted claws, seasoned raw ears of croaker, sea bass, yellow tail, flatfish, sweetfish in soy sauce, broiled scales of octopus and sea slug, beef cutlets made with pork, pork cutlets made with beef, globefish soup, chestnuts (raw and boiled), apples, pear seeds dried and wrapped in gold paper, bananas, pineapples, sweetened fig petals, rice candies containing methadone, frog egg soup, green bean jelly, vegetable gelatin,

Field-fruit wine, Suntory, cinnamon flavored distilled spirits, champagne, pine wine, dry gin, plum wine, aralia wine, Johnny Walker, White Horse, Napolean Cognac, refined and unrefined liquors, distilled spirits, *Sake*, Chinese liquor, vodka, and rum.

Forgetting to shut his mouth and with spittle drooling out, the prosecutor general sighed: "Aah, such good fortunes are the rewards of banditry! If I had but known this, I would have joined them long before. My conscience has surely been my worst enemy."

One of the five bandits sidled up to the prosecutor general inviting him to eat and drink with them. Never had he tasted such delicious food! Never had he drunk such good-tasting wine! At first he ate and drank in moderation, but soon without control, like a pig. Becoming drunk, but still master over his tongue, he scrambled to his feet to make a speech.

Chewing, spitting and making a lot of noise, he nevertheless spoke in a grave and dignified voice.

"Dear fortunate and honorable bandits!
"I believe that you should not be punished for your crimes. Instead our society should be blamed and held responsible for the deeds you have committed.
"You are not bandits, but respectable robbers who are the faithful servants of our society! It is my deepest desire that you should continue on your trodden way."

The bandits responded with shouts and laughter, slapping each other on the back. The prosecutor general ran out and arrested the young peasant, binding his hands behind his back and saying: "I arrest you for having falsely accused these five servants of the people."

Twilight had come. With the sun setting on the western hill, the lonely wild goose had found her partner and the waxing moon cast its light over the earth.

Pushing the helpless young peasant, who had starved in *Cholla-Do*,
  who had come to Seoul to seek his fortune,
  who had been oppressed by everyone,
  who was ending up in jail,
the drunken prosecutor general returned to his
  office with unsteady steps.

There was nobody who would help the young peasant.

There was nobody who could help the young peasant.

Good luck!
Good bye!

The five bandits thanked the prosecutor general for his courage. They rewarded him with a house guarded by dogs next to their own residences. With a deep sense of achievement, the prosecutor general had the most sophisticated weapons at his disposal to guard the bandits' properties, while enjoying his life in a grande style.

But one beautiful late morning, stretching himself

out luxuriously in bed, he was struck dead by a lightning bolt.

The five bandits were struck down at the same time, and bled from the six orifices of the body.[24]

Such incidents have been occurring for a long time and are on everyone's lips. I, a poor poet, merely attempt to pass the story on.

1. Korea's highest mountain, located on the China-Korea border. It has long served as a symbol of Korea.

2. The legendary forebear of the Korean people, said to have founded Korea on Mt. Paektu in the year 2,300 B.C.

3. A murderer who received wide news coverage after killing a great number of people in the outskirts of Seoul.

4. A new Seoul suburb.

5. Wealthy districts of Seoul.

6. The most prestigious streets of the city.

7. The mountain situated at the center of Seoul.

8. A legendary animal, huge and tough-skinned.

9. The poet spells out the Korean words for tycoon (*chaebol*), Assemblyman (*Kukhoeuiwon*), government official (*kogup-kongmuwon*), general (*changsong*) and minister (*chang-ch'agwan*) using old Chinese ideographs that are homophonic with the Korean pronunciation but which denote "a pack of mad dogs," "hunchbacked foxes and dogs snarling at monkeys," "meritless pigs seated on mountaintops," "gorillas," and "mad dogs winking at the rising sun," respectively.

10. Somewhat more than 50 tons.

11. U.S.$1 = 396 *Won*

12. A great magician referred to in Chinese literature.

13. An ancient Chinese warrior of evil ways, whose eyes were little more than narrow slits and have become synonymous with slyness.

14. The collapse of *Wawoo* Apartments in April 1970 was

attributed to cheap and faulty construction on the part of Seoul's Bureau of Construction. Seoul's mayor was relieved of his duties as a result of the accident, which claimed some 128 lives.

15. One Chong In Suk was murdered by her brother early in 1970 because of her alleged immorality. It was later discovered that she had been on intimate terms with various high government officials and was privy to a great many state secrets.

16. A small Japanese-made car assembled in Korea.

17. A Chinese general famous for his heavy whiskers.

18. A diminutive used to underscore the Korean people's helplessness.

19. *Chongno* 3rd Street and *Yang-Dong* are centers of prostitution, *Myong-Dong* is a luxury center, *Mugyo-Dong* is an entertainment center, *Ch'onggyech'On* is a slum, and *Wangsim-Ni* is a human-waste disposal area in Seoul.

20. A legendary river along whose banks men are said to live happy lives.

21. The poet uses the polite and vulnerable *Cholla-Do* dialect.

22. A newly built Seoul suburb for wealthy military officers.

23. A general known for his courage who defended Korea against Chinese invasion in the seventeenth century.

24. A miserable form of death believed reserved only for the most evil of men.

Groundless Rumors

I. Origin of a Sound

Since not too long ago in the town of Seoul
A strange sound repeating itself incessantly has
    been heard,
A strange weird sound.
There are some people who, each time they hear
    the sound, shake
Like an aspen leaf and shed cold sweat.
It is even more strange because these people are
    money bags
Who can shit giant turds.
Kung . . .
That's it . . . Kung
What's that sound?
Is that the sound of a tear gas bomb exploding?
    No! Kung . . .
Is it the sound of a war breaking out, of a nuclear
    explosion, of Hirohito[1] farting? No!
Is it the sound of Nixon belching? No.
Is it the sound of Chinese Communist Army salute
    guns welcoming the big-nosed Americans at
    Tienanmen Square in Peking? No.
What is it then?
Kung . . . listen to it . . . Kung . . . there
    it is . . . Kung
Does anybody know where that sound comes
    from? Kung . . . Kung . . .

Now listen people to the source of that sound.
It does not come from Russia or America or China
    or Japan but from the Republic of Korea,
From the eastern part of Seoul,
Where life is tough amidst flying dust and if you
    go past *Chong yang–ri*[2] and continue farther
There runs a stream blacker than coal,
The stink of its rotting water penetrating the air,
    and on its long, long embankment
Shack houses in rows and in clusters clinging to
    one another and creaking
Squeaking, creaking,
Swaying before the wind to and fro, left and right,
The swinging squeaking shacks.

In one corner in one of the shacks,
In a cramped rented room, lived a fellow named
    An-Do[3]
Who had come from the countryside hoping to
    make it in the big city,
Working as hard as an ox,
Timid as a mouse,
Obedient as a sheep.
He was an innocent and decent man who could
    live without laws telling him how to behave,
But because of some evil bondage from a previous
    existence or some wicked bad luck that must
    have come into his life,
None of his plans succeeded.
Sometimes a glimpse of hope . . . but again
    failure.

Others seemed to thrive
But not he.
Not even a love affair, not to mention a marriage,
Not even finding a room to rent, let alone
    buying a house.
He searched everywhere to find a job.
He didn't succeed.
He hoped his luck would change,
But it didn't.
Day after day passed by . . .
Failure —
Because of no backer; because of no school ties;
    because of no cash to buy a position;
Because of no money for bribes.
Alone and no one helping, even a tiny
    shop couldn't make it.
He cried. He squirmed. He raged.
But all in vain.
In desperation he resigned himself to his fate.
But even then he did not succeed.

Tried to hang himself—but there was no rafter
    to tie the rope to,
Tried to inhale the fumes of coal smoke—but the
    paper covering the window frames had too
    many holes,
Tried to poison himself by swallowing potassium
    cyanide in cheap wine, but there was no money
    to buy wine, in vain, in vain, in vain.
Neither resisting, nor even shouting, nor
    resting—even for a moment—was permitted.

For him to stand on his own two feet
    was not permitted under any circumstances.

If he had had the guts to stand up firmly on his
    own two feet even just once
He would have been charged with all kinds of
    crimes which nobody
Had ever heard of or seen or even imagined.

What else could he do but run
Day and night, day in day out,
Run this way run that way, and what did he get
    for it: nothing, only running.
Run horizontally, run vertically, forwards,
    backwards, and even stand on his head:
    nothing, only running.

If he earned ten *won,* a hundred *won* were taken
    away; if he earned a hundred *won,* a thousand
    won were taken away.
Every day of the year without exception he was
    harassed and harassed and harassed by this guy
    and that guy, guy with government power,
    guy with sweet talk, guy with strong fists,
    guy with powerful backing, guy with the
    letter "B" for bureaucrat written on his
    forehead, guy with the letter "T" for tax
    collector written on the bridge of his nose,
    guy with "swindler" written in his smiling
    eyes and fast-talking mouth, guy with "fraud"
    written on his gold teeth.

He was surrounded by cats of the worst breed.
Harassed, chewed, beaten, kicked, bloodied,
 trampled,
Even the trainfare left for going back home, which
 he had so carefully
Folded and hidden in his underwear, had been
 taken away.
So totally exhausted was he, more dead then
 alive . . . more dead than alive . . . more dead
 than alive . . .
To be drafted into the homeguard to do his duty
 for the fatherland
Surrounded by slogans like "Espionage!" "Enemy
 Planes!"
I will undergo the training, he said.
"No, you can't."
"Why not?"
"Cut your hair."
"I have no money to get it cut."
It never stopped.
"Remove your shack."
"How can I, it doesn't belong to me?"
"Three "un's," five "no's."⁴
"Pay your taxes in advance, for this and for that."
"I can't. I would rather end my life by drowning
 myself in a piss pot."
"No, you cannot end your life."
It never stopped.
Money for rice, money for the collection of night
 soil, money for water, money for electricity,
 and on and on.

Money for room, money for clothes, for shoes,
    for medicine, for side dishes, for soy sauce,
Money for coal, and on and on and on.
Money for wine, money for tea, for newspapers,
    for books, for haircuts, bathing, cigarettes,
    and on and on.
Money for congratulations and on top of it
Money for condolence
Money for contributions and on top of it
Money for the local office and on top of it
Money for transportation
And on top of it money for the creditor, and on
    top of it and on top of it . . .
Endless expectations, totally in bondage.
What could he do?
What else, other than to keep running like a mad
    dog,
To have enough not to starve but not enough to
    die.
He kept running like a little tiger whose tail
    was afire.

With one foot on the ground and the other foot
    raised in the air,
With one foot raised and the other foot touching
    the ground,
This foot on the ground and that foot raised,
That foot raised, this foot on the ground,
Tipping this way, tipping that way,
Stamping, leaping.
Each day he set out looking for work,

Offering himself as an errand boy at the real
      estate office, a messenger boy at the security
      office, a servant at the mutual finance office,
      a janitor at the trade business office.
He offered himself as a factory hand at
      the textile factory, a fire man at the
      metal casting factory, a dispatcher at the
      sugar factory, a handy-man at the clothing
      factory.
He peddled soup on *Ita-won* Street, radish leaves
      at *Tapsim-ni*, peddled in *Namdaemun*
      Market, hustled poisonous swellfish eggs
      in *Tongdaemun* Market,
Became a dirt carrier at a construction site for
      A-frames,
A vegetable salesman at *Morsenae*,
An extra in movies.
Dashing to the left, to the right, rushing headlong
      to the east and the west and to the south
      and north,
helter-skelter, hurry-scurry.
Tired and exhausted, starved and sickened,
One day while the sun was setting
He put his two feet on the ground and cried out:
"What a bitch this world is!"

No sooner had the words left his mouth than
Handcuffs were put on An-Do's hands and he was
      dragged to court.
Pounding his gavel three times,

The judge opened the hearing.

"What's the charge?"

"His crime is that of standing on his own two feet
and spreading groundless rumors, Sir."

"Aah, that is a big crime indeed."

"The accused, by standing on the ground with
his two feet and spreading groundless rumors,
committed the crime of touching the ground
with his two feet, the crime of resting his
body, the crime of tranquilizing his mind, the
crime of attempting to stand up despite his
poverty-stricken status, the crime of wasting
time in thinking, the crime of looking up
at the sky without a feeling of shame, the
crime of

Inhaling the air and expanding his thorax, the
crime of forgetting his status and standing
upright which is granted only to the special
privileged class, the crime of insolently
avoiding the national policies for more
production, export, and construction without
a moment's rest, the crime of violating the
3 "un's," 5 "no's," 7 "anti's," 9 "non's," the
crime of

Thinking up groundless rumors which would
mislead innocent people, the crime of
intending to voice the same rumors, the crime
of voicing the same, the crime of intending
to spread the same, the crime of spreading
the same, the crime of disrespecting the

fatherland, the crime of disgracing his native
language, the crime of comparing the
fatherland to an animal, the crime of creating
a possibility for the world to look on the
fatherland as an animal, the crime of
Disturbing the environment for capital investment,
the crime of promoting social disorder and
creating social unrest, the crime of agitating
the mind of the people, the crime of growing
weary of life, the crime of escaping from
existing customs, the crime of
Possibly helping the enemy, the crime of
entertaining anti-establishment thought, the
crime of possibly organizing an
anti-government body through telepathic
means, the crime of anti-government riot
conspiracy, the crime of strong mindedness,
and on top of it the crime of violating the
special society manipulating law.

"GUILTY," the judge declared,
Pounding his gavel three more times.
"And it is hereby solemnly declared in
accordance with the Law
That from the body of the accused shall be cut
off immediately, after the closing of this court,
One head, so that he may not be able to think
up or spread groundless rumors anymore,
Two legs, so that he may not insolently stand on
the ground on his two feet any more,

One penis and two testicles, so that he may not
    produce another, seditious like himself.
And after this is done, since there exists a great
    danger of his attempting to
Resist, his two hands shall be tied together behind
    his back, his trunk shall be
Tied with a wet leather vest, and his throat shall
    be stuffed with a hard and long-lasting
    voice-preventing tool, and then he shall be
    placed in confinement
For five hundred years from this date."

"No!" he cries out.
Snip
"No, my penis is gone!" snip snap
"My testicles too, no, no." crack
"My neck, oh my neck is gone." hack hack
"No, my two legs also gone." Handcuffs, leather
    vest, voice-preventing tool.
So they brutally shoved the fellow An-Do
    into a solitary cell.
Click
The locks were locked, and while the locking
    sound echoed farther and
    farther he continued to cry,
"No, no, no, no. What has been done to me?
"I was clad in rags and starved, worked,
"Beaten and oppressed, but did not utter a word
    of protest.
"I didn't rest, didn't lie down, didn't even sleep,

"And yet what have they done to me?

"What devilish crime did I commit to bring upon
me a punishment so severe?

"You wild geese flying up in the sky, do you know
how I feel?

"Can you tell me whether my mother is standing
on the new road near our shack

"Waiting for my return?

"Is she weeping soundlessly, looking in the
direction of Seoul, wearing her out-of-season
clothes?

"Wild geese, tell my mother

"I will return,

"I will return even if I am dead—

"Even if my body is torn into one thousand or ten
thousand pieces.

"I will break out through the walls of this jail,
I'll leap over the fence

"Even if I have to sell my soul to the devil.

"I will return, mother, whatever happens, I will
return."

And then An-Do wanted to sing, but he had no
head. He wanted to cry, but he had no eyes.

He wanted to shout, but he had no voice.

With neither voice nor tears, he cried soundlessly
day after day, night after night, shedding
blood-red tears,

Crying soundlessly in the depths of his soul, crying
no, no, no.

Roll,

Roll your trunk.

An-Do rolled over and over,
Back and forth from wall to wall, Kung, back
and forth from wall to wall, continuously,
Kung
And one more time Kung and again
Kung
Kung
Kung
And there were powerful people who had money
and who could shit giant turds who trembled
each time they heard that sound;
Who could not fall asleep each time they heard
that sound, overcome by a terrible fear.
They gave the order to execute An-Do at once.
But the sound persisted,
Kung.

A strange and mysterious thing, that Kung
sound is driving some people mad; it never
stops.
Yes, it is strange indeed.
It is heard even now, day and night.
Some people say it is the work of a ghost,
Others that it is An-Do who did not die but is
still alive, somewhere,
rolling his trunk from wall to wall . . .
The latter, as they whisper this story in the
streets of Seoul, have a strange fire in their
eyes.

II. Ko Kwan[5]

A Communist spy has horns and a long tail,
     hairy hands
And a body as red as a red radish.
A prize is given to any man who reports or
     captures a person of said appearance.

On a Christmas eve, bells jingling in the distance,
Snow coming down quietly,
Ko-Kwan puts on his clothes.
He starts with U.S.-made jockey shorts and
     undershirt
As white as snow,
Then long woolen underwear, camel hair socks
     and a white shirt, white as the snow,
     "Daimaru" or "Takashimaya" brand,[6]
A necktie bought in Paris, Chinese green jade cuff
     links, as green as China's West Lake,
Scottish tweed pants,
And a crocodile belt from the Congo. ———
Oh! I forgot cologne. One drop of "Tabu"!
Then his vest,
Then a jacket with a daffodil handkerchief in
     the breast pocket,
A dark soft double-overcoat,
Then a deep-red wool muffler, red as blood,
A soft Feodora, British-made,
Blue snow-glasses.
Oh! and his wristwach, a Rado 21,
A white gold ring on his finger, black kangaroo-

skin gloves on his hands, black cordovan
    shoes.
Then he gets into his black-as-a-black-leapord
    eight-cylinder Mercedes Benz 71.

On a Christmas eve, bells jingling in the distance,
Snow coming down quietly,
The Mercedes stops at a flower shop.
The Mercedes leaves the flower shop.
The Mercedes stops at a hotel.
Ko-Kwan enters the big hotel slowly.
"Welcome, your Excellency!"
"Oh, no! Please don't call me your Excellency!"
"We are very much honored!
"We can imagine how your Excellency is busy
    with the modernization of the country!"
"Tonight I am a commoner. Ha ha ha!"
"This hotel is the symbol of the modernization
    of our country."
"Well done, well done, well done."
"Thank you, Sir. She is waiting, your Excellency."
"I know, I know, I know."
Brightly lit chandeliers, resembling those of
    Versailles,
Carpets on the floor, tapestries on the walls,
A Velasquez,
Beside it a huge Yi dynasty painting of the
    "Procession of the Governor of Pyongyang,"
Under it ancient Korean ceramics displayed in a
    huge glass case,
Beside them a Mexican shell, an amethyst, an Inca

stone statue and masks—
The mask of a god, of a leper, masks of many
    kinds—
Korean classic wind and string instruments on
    display,
Beside them lacquer jewel boxes, Yi dynasty, and
    a black folding fan, rococo style.

Ko-Kwan rides the elevator.
He nudges the elevator girl's hip, she like a
    blooming flower,
Squeezing her buttocks, laughing smugly.
The girl swings with the soft music of Satchmo,
    Adam, Montant,
Bartant, and Tom Jones.
Orchids, begonias, oranges, coconut trees, plum
    flowers line the long corridor.
And over there a couple in white clothes
Whisper, talk, giggle, laugh, and run.
Fade.
Next, a grey-haired elderly gentleman accompanying
    a young girl wearing a blue scarf
Fades.
Next. Oh! What beautiful white skin she has!
A fascinating lady, a black veil hiding her face,
    with a young boy wearing a pretty blue jacket
Fade.
What is next?
Only the night crying out for solitude.
Ko-Kwan fondles the elevator girl's bosom,

laughing, while she guides him to one of the
    doors.
Ko-Kwan opens the door of the room.
"Oh, Tower-up!" (Let's call her "Tower-up.")
"Good evening, Mademoiselle Tower-up!
"How about these flowers? Aren't they elegante?"
"Good evening, Sir! Yes, they are really
    elephante.
Do you like me?"
"Yes, I like you. You are graceful but look sad."
"Your Excellency is handsome."
"Thank you. How about a drink?"
"Yes, please."
"Champagne?"
"No, whiskey."
"You seem melancholy."
"What kind of *Kholi*,[7] Sir?"
"You look . . . mmm . . . classic? Modern?
    Anyway, you have a delicate, romantic and
    passionate air."
"You, too, your Excellency."
"Now let's toast to your melancholy."
"To your Excellency's health."
"Come close to me."
"I feel shy."
"Come close to me."
"If you don't mind."
"My cute little squirrel. My sorrow. My joy. My
    all. Your eyes are like shining black pearls.
    Your skin . . ."

"Your Excellency has nice lips."
"Your dark hair is like the sea at night. Your
    skin . . ."
"I feel like weeping."
"Your skin is like . . ."
"I love you, Sir."
"Turn off the lights."
"Yes, Sir."
"Come close to me."

On a Christmas eve, bells jingling in the distance,
Snow coming down quietly,
Night deepens, this night more precious than
    white pearls. This night. The snow covering
    the earth.
Midnight! Fire!
Fire! Fire! Fire!
FaFaFaFaFaFaFaFaFaFire!
Somebody may have pissed in bed! Fire!
Somebody may have played with matches! Fire!
Somebody must be talking in his sleep! Fire!
Wait! This is the real thing! Hot flames burning
    brightly!
Somebody rushes to the door.
Somebody crawls to the door.
Somebody rushes to the toilet door, mistaking
    it for the door to the hall.
Somebody hides under the bed, thinking that
    the fire won't reach him there.
Men and women, having slept in the same room,
Run separately like strangers from each other:

Men to the east! women to the west!
Women desperately running to the west turn back
    and run to the east, knowing that the west
    quarter is on fire.
Men run east and, turning back, run to the west:
They bump into each other head-on and fall to
    the floor on their asses.
They can't get out! A man sits down and laments
    loudly:
"I've lost face! I will lose my position!"
The woman beside him farts loudly, laughs
    foolishly and lies down on the bed. Fire! Fire!
This stud shouts "Fire!" That slut shouts "Fire!"
Everybody shouts "Fire!"
They think they can escape the fire by shouting fire.
Completely naked men and women rush without
    shame in groups like herds from this corner
    to that corner. Crying, help, help, help.
A women puts her head into the closet and waves
    both hands like a traffic policeman.
A man clasps his balls carefully with both hands
    while his teeth rattle rhythmically, tadak,
    tadak, tadak.
A public official wearing only a dog tag,
A girl wearing only a pearl necklace,
A guy wearing a pistol on his naked body,
A guy who asks anyone who will listen, what he
    should do,
Telling them that under any circumstances he has to
    get on the Northwest Orient flight tomorrow
    because he is a State Department grantee.

77

A guy faints after shitting several times.
A woman crying with a frowning face,
A woman shrieking again and again,
A girl proudly pinning her college emblem on her
    panties, otherwise naked, ignoring the
    emergency,
A naked guy walking around wearing his precious
    Tokyo hat,
A guy clutching a bag of money, while still
    searching frantically for it,
A guy just enjoying watching the young girls,
A girl covering her face with a muffler leaving
    two holes for her eyes,
A guy covering his face with the same,
A couple walking in an embrace like Siamese twins,
An old guy and a young girl, who, without being
    asked, answer "This is my daughter-in-law"
    and "This is my father-in-law,"
"Didn't we discuss business all night without
    sleeping, my dear?"
Nodding to one another.
A guy and a girl quarreling with each other, saying
"It's your fault. It's you who ruined me."
A guy trying to push away his terrified girl who
    hangs on to him,
A thief stealing enthusiastically,
A fellow collecting everything he can set eyes upon,
A fellow putting everything into his pockets.
This fellow, that guy, this girl, that woman, all
    are naked.

High official and cheap slut; old man and young
   girl; young man and old woman; company
   president and his young secretary; society
   woman and giggolo; college girl and college
   boy; swindler and high official's wife; playboy
   and pimp; son of high official and rich man's
   daughter; wanton woman and sex crazy boy;
   Lolita; Adonis; Japanese; Koreans.
All of them, struggling to escape, running from
   one corner to the other seeking frantically
   for an exit, crying.
Then light bulbs pop; liquor bottles explode;
   windows crack; iron beams heave; fireballs
   fly; lights flash; trees burn; walls crumble;
   carpets burn; everything burning.
The universe is trembling. Thunder rends the sky.
All is over.
A steel reinforced building in the end is no safer
   than a poor farmer's house of thatch.
Everything was destroyed, blasted, folded, cut
   and bent.
Everything was burnt and twisted.
They did not try to put out the fire. They just ran
   to escape from the fire in the building where
   all the exits were locked.
They run into each other. "You son of a bitch,
   your eyes are merely for decoration, eh!"
He drew back to strike the naked man hard, but
   he saw that the man was his father.
"Daddy, how come you're here?"

"You good-for-nothing, leave me alone."
In this confusion, a stud chasing a slut squeezed
    the ass of another woman.
Who in the hell is bothering me now?"
She intended to curse the stud, but finds it is her
    husband.
"Oh my goodness, what brought you here?"
Tit for tat.

Fire ladders were extended higher and higher,
    and water from fire hoses arced higher and
    higher
But they couldn't reach the fire.
A helicopter flew lower and lower, dropped a rope,
But too far from the roof and flew away again.
More water, more ladders. But all failed.
More fire trucks came. More helicopters flew over
    the scene.
But they fell back.
"Hmmm, this must be an emergency."
"That's an idea. Let's go to the emergency
    staircase."
"Damn, you are so stupid! There is no emergency
    staircase in this building."
"Why not?"
"Don't you know that they bribed the fire
    inspector so they wouldn't have to install an
    emergency staircase?"
"Let's go to the roof."
"You crazy idiot. All the ways leading to the roof
    are blocked. Don't you know why?

To prevent guests from running away without
    paying their bills."
"Open the fire plug."
"You idiot. It's only for show."
"Why?"
"Ha ha ha ha, just for show. They bribed the other
    fire inspector."
"Let's go down then!"
"You are as mad as the State of Emergency
    Decrees![8]
"You will die if you go down."
"Why?"
"Ha ha ha. Don't you know that fire burns from
    the bottom up?"
"Then what shall we do?"
"You damn, damn fool, you will perish like others
    who have died on the stake before you."

People were killed in the fire; burnt, trampled,
    crushed; some were electrocuted; some died
    face up and some face down; some suffocated;
    some died from burns on their asses, others
    on their guts; some jumped from windows
    and died of broken bones and snapped spines.
Some died exhausted. Some died shitting.
Some died laughing, crying, shrieking, sitting,
    standing, running, bragging, quaking,
    clenching their fists, lying on their bellies,
    lying under a girl's belly, kissing, kneading,
    massaging, sucking, touching a girl; dressing;
Some died quietly, unwillingly, honorably,

shamefully, poorly, or gentlemen-like.

Among the dying, some Japanese shouted "Is this
modernization?

"Is the lack of an emergency staircase
modernization?

"Eat shit, you fools! Some modernization," and
plunged to hell.

A guy barely pulled himself up to the window and
shouted: "Damn it! I have to die without
spending a single one of my billions of *won*
deposited in a Swiss bank account."

Tear drops fell like chicken shit on his cheek as
he dropped back into the fire.

An old woman and a giggolo, exhausted after a
night of love-play, plunged down together.

A young college girl and a big-bellied old man
leaped out together.

Another couple jumped out naked and descended
through the wind to hell.

A woman, her hair bedraggled, wanted to sing her
last song,

A Japanese song she had learned for the purpose
of visiting Japan, regardless of the situation.

She sang "blue and white neon signs twinkle . . ."
and died as the blue and white neon signs
twinkled outside.

Many people were dead, and more and more were
about to die in one way or another.

Beside Ko-Kwan, who was looking for the right
spot to jump from, sidled a woman with
tussled hair, naked and burnt red;

She saw a long ugly tail dangling behind Ko-Kwan,
     who was also naked and burnt red.
She was astonished to see the tail and pulled it
     hard with both her hands.
She said: "Oh my goodness, you have a tail."
"What? A tail? You dirty whore. Hands off."
"You want to escape alone? If you leave me, I will
     expose your secret to a weekly magazine, that
     Ko-Kwan has a tail growing out of his ass."
"What? A weekly magazine? You dirty slut, go
     to hell!"
Then he kicked her and, leaving her there, plunged
     through the window.
Fortunately he fell on a thatched roof where snow
     had piled up, close to the hotel, tumbling
     several times.
But he was alive, and stood up.
Now, the spectators saw a red body with a long
     ugly tail landing on that little thatched roof
     and they thought it must be a Communist spy.
"Spy! Catch him!" they shouted. And they ran
     after him with iron bars and shovel handles.
Astonished, Ko-Kwan ran and ran, covering his
     face and gripping his tail in fear of being
     caught.
Ko-Kwan has been running ever since, running
     naked, desperate, down the back alleys of
     Seoul.
That is what people are whispering.

III. Adoration of a Six-Shooter

One day in the year of the pig, the King held a
     banquet.
A long snake coiled in the rafters of the hall, then
     suddenly disappeared. Later the King fell ill,
     his belly swelling more each day.
Medicines prescribed by Western doctors didn't
     work at all,
So the King consulted a shaman living deep in
     the mountains far away.
"Tell me what kind of disease I suffer from,"
     asked the King after he explained his
     condition.
The shaman, having listened to the King's words,
     blinked twice, twisted his finger, and
     mumbled hocus-pocus,
Then whispered into the King's ear:
"Your majesty is pregnant."
"What? What do you say? Pregnant? How can
     a man be pregnant?"
"I beg your pardon, Your Majesty. But you are
     carrying an egg, the egg of a snake."
"What? An egg of a snake?"
"I am sorry, I am sorry your Majesty."
"Ooh, what a disgrace! What shall I do?"
The shaman whispered into the King's ear again:
"Shut everybody's mouth tightly. Stop anyone
     from coming into your room, then take the
     potion I will prescribe to induce abortion."
"What is it?"

"I recommend that Your Majesty eat 30 million
livers of live humans.

"Best of all are the livers of Communists, known
to be the most bitter. But lately they have all
been devoured and are therefore hard to
come by.

"Second best are the livers of live Christians.
Moreover, since they are spreading a rumor
that Your Majesty is miraculously pregnant,
by eating their livers you will be killing two
birds with one stone."

Soon after, the King ordered the most well-known
Christians to assemble in a small church.

The King addressed them:

"Hear me, ye Jesus peddlers! You are humbly born
and have transgressed against the teaching of
your ancestors. Ever since I became King,
I have permitted you to earn your living,
solely by my magnificent grace. Unless you are
mean beasts, you should be deeply grateful
to me.

"Recently I fell ill and became so emaciated that my
skin touched bone. Since I was told that your
livers will cure my disease, you had better
cut open your bellies and dedicate them to
curing my illness so that you may repay the
benevolence which your King has bestowed
upon you.

"I further order that, after doing so, you sew your
mouths closed. If you dare to speak of this,
we will consider it a crime—misleading

society and deceiving the people—and your
family and relatives shall perish."

The instant the King finished his speech, from a
corner of the church a sharp voice cried,
"Go to hell."

Enraged, the King thrust his right hand into his
inside pocket, but held himself in check
because he needed their livers.

"I am your King. I have a conscience, and I have
my honor. Do you think I will eat your livers
forever?

"If and when I have recovered, at an appropriate
time, I will return them to you. Don't worry,
don't worry."

Before the King had finished speaking, a husky
voice from another corner of the church cried,
"Stop telling lies!"

Now, it is known that pregnancy generally causes
nervousness. The King boiled with fury. He
could control himself no longer. He pulled a
black six-shooter from his inside pocket and
pointed it at the assembled Christians.

"Have you anything further to say?"

Only laughter here and there. "We are not afraid
of guns. Shoot us. Shoot us. It's only a toy
gun anyway. Shoot us."

The King wanted to shoot them, all of them. But
he needed their livers to cure his disease.
He was furious.

Bang!

He fired a blank.

He looked around proudly. But no one blinked.
　　Everyone just continued talking, showing no
　　fear. Discouraged, the King looked around
　　the church and spotted a very small statue of
　　Jesus on the Cross.
"Aah. Now I have it.
"Your fearlessness comes from that statue.
"The most hated thing in the world is that cursed
　　Jesus.
"He pretended to bear all the burdens and agony
　　of human beings.
"He was humbly born, a carpenter.
"But he was ambitious.
"By calling himself the Son of Heaven,
"He misled the world and confused the people
　　by means of promises and rumors.
"He deserved blame and he deserved death.
"He lacked due appreciation for the power
　　of Rome.
"It's not Jesus the people should depend on, but
　　the six-shooter.
"Listen, I will destroy you with my six-shooter!"
Bang!
Blood spurted high into the air from the bosom
　　of Jesus and flowed on endlessly.
Blood filled the church.
The Jesus peddlers rose up and wailed.
Suddenly the astonished King cried out, his body
　　writhing, as out dropped a yellow snake egg;
　　its shell cracked and out slithered a baby
　　snake crying, "Mama, Mama."

The King screamed and fired his gun again and
     again.
"Close the four great gates," he shouted.
"No one may leave.
"Arrest them all.
"I decree a new law forbidding freedom of speech.
"Bring in the troops.
"Bring in the air force.
"Bring in the Palace guards.
"Crush and grind that statue of Jesus into powder."
The rifles went bang, bang, bang.
The machine guns: ta-ta-ta.
The cannons: boom-boom.
The tanks: booooom.
The planes: zoom, zoom, zoom.
Standing in a circle, all at once
They fired ta-ta-ta, ta-ta-ta.
But none of the bullets reached or touched the
     small statue of Jesus;
Instead
The bullets criss-crossed,
Killing and crushing the troops
Until, at last, all had perished.
Such a story is whispered in the streets of Seoul.
Now wise men have long said that misfortune
     begins with the misunderstanding of auguries,
And that the use of arms and murderous weapons
     is not the way to happiness, but the first step
     to self-destruction.
Our story bears witness to the truth of the wise
     men's sayings.

1. The present Emperor of Japan.

2. A street in the eastern part of Seoul.

3. The Chinese ideographs used to write this name denote "a peaceful way." An-Do thus implies an easy-going, compliant nature.

4. The "three un's" refer to a set of social ills which Prime Minister Kim Jong Pil, in a speech before the National Assembly in 1971, claimed he wanted to wipe out: *un*rest, *un*trust, and *un*justice. The "five no's" refer to public attitudes that the Prime Minister declared he wanted to change: no-concern, no-spirit, no-responsibility, no-consciousness, and no-conception.

5. The Korean word *ko-kwan* means "high official." The poet spells it out using old Chinese ideographs which are homophonic with the Korean pronunciation but actually denote "the view from the horse's ass."
   The Ko-Kwan story refers to the mysterious Daeyunkak Hotel fire of Christmas Eve, 1971. Husbands and wives and fathers and sons are known to have been lost in the conflagration, but many of the victims remain unidentified for reasons of "face." It was widely rumored that the hotel, a fire trap, was owned by President Chung Hee Park and former head of the KCIA Lee Hu-rak.

6. Well-known Japanese department stores with branches throughout Asia.

7. *Kholi* is Korean for "an animal's tail." The poet is ridiculing the self-conscious and widely misinformed use of English and other foreign words by the Korean *nouveaux riches*.

8. A reference to President Park's "state of emergency," which is used to justify his authoritarian rule.

Cry of the People

Hear our cry! Hear our cry!
Crying out of aching hunger.

Patience quickly running out!
Can we long believe this ruler?

Bodies weary from low wages
Now are dying of high prices.

Will we see "Abundant Eighties,"
Or first be downed by gnawing hunger?

The world's oil crisis shrilly blamed
For a nation's economic ruin.

Empty trickery no more—
Give up power, before you fall!

The *Yushin* signboard advertisement[1]
Is merely to deceive the people;

On democratic constitution's tomb
Dictatorship has been established;

Human rights went up in smoke;
Now sheer survival is at stake.

The people's leaders thrown in prison
For espousing democratic rights.

For their deep belief in freedom
Students and Christians are labelled "traitors";

Rule by fear and violence
Shows total desperation.

Resign in a peaceful manner!
Your rule is breaking down.

May 16[2] was political violence —
Let us examine the traitorous act.

Under Japanese colonial rule,
As an officer you killed our patriots;[3]

Under Yankee military rule
You slavishly curried favor.

The flower almost bloomed in April;
The blossom crushed by *coup d'état*.[4]

They say a virgin can find
Excuse for being pregnant;

Traitors too can find good slogans
For traitorous usurpation.

Up went the anti-Communist banner;
"Eliminate Corruption" was the cry.

The trumpet of promises sounded good
To solve the problems of survival;

But return to civilian rule
Changed nothing but the uniform.[5]

Modernization! Nation-building!
Nicknames for foreign power's yoke.

Korea's treaty with Japan
Swung wide the door of treason.[6]

Foreign capital seduced us;
Our economy was raped.

A privileged few aquire wealth,
Corruption surpassing that of old.

Ceaseless progress! The law is scrapped
For a dynasty's perpetuation.[7]

Development's main purpose:
To rationalize dictatorship;

"Abundant Seventies" never found
Except in propaganda's prattle.

A rising cry for a change of power
Grows among the common folk;

But "stability without chaos"
Holds the people's will in check.

Militia drills at work and study,
Scare the public with false crises;

Dissatisfaction is increasing;
Exploding is the people's anger.

"National Harmony", "National Security"
Are now habitual slogans;

But a widening gap between rich and poor
Denies harmonious progress;

Rather the oppressive order
Amplifies the chaos.

Dietmen are merely puppets
Caring only for their babes;[8]

Jurists appointed by the ruler
Become his ruthless henchmen;

Assemblymen, carefully chosen,
Toady to the leader;

Manifesting fascist spirit,
Farewell to democracy.

The people rise up in defiance,
The naked ruler stands alone.

Anti-Communist, security laws
Brand writers, intellectuals as spies.

Under the guise of lawful rule,
Evil laws spread their dominion;

Economy mortgaged and surrendered
To maintain oppressive tyranny;

The economy quakes and trembles
Before the smallest crisis.

Don't hide economic subjugation,
Taking refuge in the world's oil crisis.

The ruler has ruined the economy:
This the people know.

In economic co-operation's name
Our economy is colonized;

Economic independence but a distant vision;
Unification a receding dream.

The debt transcends five billion;
Loans get ever harder.

To Southeast Asia and to Europe,
Our begging mission wanders;

Pitiful is our destiny;
Worldwide beggars we've become.

Famous as an export nation,
Our deficit of trade increases;

For the export trade in stone,
Even tomb stones are not sacred.[9]

When export reaches to ten billion,
Will territory too be gone?[10]

Favoring aid grains from abroad,
Agriculture was destroyed;[11]

Now prices abroad have soared,
The ruler knows not what to do.

In agricultural development alone
Lies healthy economic growth;

Depending solely on foreign aid
Is to build a castle out of sand.

Burn oil! Burn coal!
Zigzag vacillation![12]

Coal burner, then oil burner,
Each is wasted in turn;[13]

Scrap iron too is expensive,
Waste thereby increased.

But what of the proverb:
"Even the head of a nail"?[14]

One man's savings cannot make up
For an entire nation's waste.

In collaboration with oil men,
Refineries are established;

See the clever ruse
To extract political funds;

Expressways are built
To consume more oil;

To sell more cars,
They shout "My car,"

Crying "Use oil first, oil first,
Coal only later";

With industries oil reliant,
Oil crises mean collapse.

In the wake of unjust agreements,[15]
Profits guaranteed in advance;

Before knowing the cost of production
Profit ratios are set.

Passing beyond the limit of injustice!
How long can it be endured?

Profiteering by foreign industry
Cannot go without restriction!

To improve the investment environment,
Compradors appear;

Tax exemptions, transfer rights,
Offered like ancestral gifts;

But rights of labor brutally suppressed,
Special laws are written;[16]

Industrial zones, export centers,
Create only regional gaps;

The logic of capital growth
Favors only big business;

Small businesses go bankrupt;
Monopoly is rampant.

For the chemical industry
Domestic capital is sought;

Burdensome taxes are exacted,
Forced savings are imposed.

Agriculture needs protection,
Funds and skills must be provided;

Devise a plan
To best cultivate the land.

Relying on imported oil,
Our coal mines left to rot;

Dependent on imports only,
Our own resources ignored;

Domestic industry lies desolate,
Dependence on foreign capital complete.

In development's name, collaboration
With foreign capital is wrought.

The policies of this regime
Can no longer be believed.

Bankrupt industry induced
To suck the blood of labor;

Pollution industries imported,
The people choked to death.[17]

The call for unification,[18]
A stream of empty words;

Dialogue with the North
But propaganda's tool;

Abusing unification,
A last ploy for self-preservation—

Foolish ruler!
Heed the warning:

Frame not the innocent as spies,
To oppress and silence their cries.

Create not incidents with the North,
To divert attention from your crimes.

No one is deceived;
The people's anger rises high.

Resign as we demand,
Your life will then be spared.

Sins against the nation
Shall not be forgiven.

The nation's strength is called for
To speed reunification;

But how can strength be built amid
Economy in ruin, a system in decay?

The road to unification lies in
Economic self-reliance, an independent state.

Betrayed by the present regime
Let us change our fate at the roots;

Labor policy said enacted
For the workers' alleged gain

Serves only industrial masters,
While workers remain enslaved.

Exposing the plight of all workers,
He burned himself to death;

Calling upon us to struggle as one,
His last words cry out in the dark;

Chon Tai Il,[19] the martyred worker,
Cries out to us still in his tomb.

The legal rights of labor
By the government undercut;

With strikes declared illegal,
The workers stay oppressed.

The dominion of evil laws
Deprives life of all its promise.

Rise up as one, five million workers!
Survival itself is at stake.

"Distribution after growth"—
Who do you think you are kidding?

Distribute now the wealth that was earned
By the workers' blood and sweat.

Bodies exhausted, home brings no rest—
Only the plague of making ends meet;

Wages defeated by price hikes;
Terrified of being dismissed.

Unite to drive out exploiters;
To secure the right to live.

Welfare funds said for the people,
Are nothing but a lie.

Keep your sugar coating
Which turns our empty stomachs.

In the name of public housing,
An apartment house is built;

Its construction cheap and shabby—
Whose life will it claim this time?

Remember *Wawoo* Apartments[20]
That heaved and collapsed in the rain?

Thoughtlessly, without reflection,
Will massacre be reenacted.

Shouting "material shortage,"
Yet busy being wasteful;

It is built and then destroyed;
Now who is profiteering?

Eight million *won* to construct it,
Seven million *won* to remove it.

By whom are the losses carried?
By the people! By the people!

Taxes cut to ease the burden,
Exacted again through indirect means;

Under the slogan of tax reform
Loopholes created, systematic exploitation;

Needed national funds are spent
Without control for political ends.

When sugar coating suddenly goes,
No one is deceived.

Squatter huts are taken down
To feign a prosperous air

When North Koreans visit,
President's daughter passes by;

This hobby of squatter hut destruction
Confuses and terrifies us all—

Driven to the city's edge
With the way cleared for Seoul's priviliged.

Jobless, workless,
How does one live?

The squatter's hut means to remain alive
Because you cannot die.

Be diligent! they say—
About what?

Be thrifty! they say—
With what?

Give me something to do:
I will work hard, be never idle;

Give me money to survive:
I will split the coin to save;

Diligence and thriftiness
Are only for the privileged;

Campaigns to save energy are
Of no concern to the poor.

The corrupt police fix their eyes
On illicit bribes alone;

With thieves and murderers rampant,
We are stricken by trembling fear.

Price checking provides excuse
To squeeze the keepers of shops.

Utilities said to be improved;
Harassing harrowed housewives.

The fountain of evil pouring forth;
What can stop the flow?

Agriculture acclaimed important;[21]
But the farmers' income falls.

The prices of tools and fertilizer soar,
While the price of grain descends.

Adhering to official lines:
The surest way to fail.[22]

The cost of feed is rising;
The price of eggs declines;

Then chickens must be sold,
And debts alone remain.

"Agricultural Co-operatives for Farmers"—
The slogan is a con!

One more official tool
To exploit the peasantry.

Fertilizer monopoly, doubly exploiting;[23]
How more cunning can you be!

Self-sufficiency a slogan only,
Food is ever short;

Imported rice has a dual price,
Undercutting the nation's harvest.[24]

To consume imported wheat,
Diversification was enforced.[25]

Diversified diet, mixed diet:
Then hunger as a diet?

Agricultural policy
Is no policy at all;

The Community Movement you trusted
Was a modernization plan;[26]

In innocence you accepted
Betrayal by the ruler.

When unknowing, keeping silence;
Even knowing, keeping still.

In silent acquiescence,
You till the soil as serfs.

But the students rose up in defiance
To voice the people's silent cry.

Accused of impure motives
Their accusations cast aside;

Their movement brutally suppressed,
As a minority dismissed;

But justice will win out,
The power of evil, fail.

Students, bulwark of democracy,
Carry on the fight!

Tigers of Anamkol! Eagles at Shinchon![27]
Stand up together to overthrow the traitor!

Joined by the people,
Advance to the front!

Smoke bombs cannot stop you,
Gun shots not deter you.

The living volcano explodes
At the Eve of Revolution . . .

With flowers in bloom,
And hearts filled with hope.

Forget not your duties,
Intellectuals and professors!

Flatter not the ruler,
When subjected to pressure!

Support them without hesitation,
When the students voice the cry!

Join them in the struggle
When the decisive moment comes.

Writers and journalists,
Join in their struggle;

Purify your pens,
For now is the time.

To overcome our common fate,
Struggle now as one.

When you first took up the pen
Was your motive not the Truth?

Reviving freedom of the press,
Let us light the torch of revolution!

Christians, independence fighters,
Betray not now the people.

In the spirit of all martyrs,
Come forth to root out evil!

You who are overloyal,
Take courage, change your hearts!

Ex-prisoners, bearing tyranny's scars,
Rise up to greet the day!

Jobless and beggars,
Struggle for survival!

Gang leaders, shoe shine boys,
Come and join the fight!

Bus drivers, train conductors,
Claim your human rights!

Opportunists, hypocrites,
You too take a stand!

Politicians, officials,
Know the people's will!

Remember October of 1973[28]—
The students' cry echoed through the land!

High school students, Christians,
Protesting together!

But oil shortage cited—
And vacation imposed.

Temporary calm on the surface,
But passions left boiling beneath.

Spring has come—the earth is waiting.
Now is the time to rise!

The will of the people is the Will of Heaven;
No one can resist it!

Who is made afraid by threat?
Who is made afraid by violence?

Better to die fighting,
Than to die of gnawing hunger.

106

Students, rise! Workers, struggle!
Farmers, join the fray!

Shake the heavens and the earth;
The spirits of our brothers will protect you.

Who can stop us? Who can slow us?
Who will block the way?

Anguished policemen sympathize;
Soldiers denounce the regime!

Absolute power corrupts absolutely;
Absolute power shall be totally destroyed!

Rise up together, stand up together,
Overthrowing the brutal rule!

In April Revolution's spirit,
Struggle on for democratic rights!

Let nothing keep us from our freedom!
Let tyranny no longer reign!

Arise, spirit of self-determination!
Guide our destiny!

And we will sing the song of peace,
In freedom, justice, and love.

1. The *Yushin* (Revitalization/Reform) Constitution was enacted by President Park on October 18, 1972. The Constitution curtails civil liberties and establishes one-man rule.

2. On May 16, 1961, Major General Chung Hee Park led a military *coup d'état* which overthrew the duly constituted civilian government of John M. Chang and Yun Po Sun.

3. Chung Hee Park is a graduate of the Japanese Imperial Army Military Academy. He served as a lieutenant in Japan's Kanto Division (Manchuria) during World War II.

4. The April flower refers to the student-inspired overthrow of the Synghman Rhee dictatorship. The post-Rhee government, stabilized under John Chang, instituted democratic reforms. Park's ascent to power reversed this trend.

5. In October 1963 Park was elected to head a civilian government.

6. Student and intellectual dissatisfaction with the Japan-Korea normalization talks, and the treaty that emerged therefrom, was widespread during the mid-1960s and persists to the present day. The terms of normalization eventually agreed upon were deemed heavily weighted in Japan's economic and diplomatic favor. The Park government, however, was primarily interested in securing financial and technological assistance for the further industrialization of South Korea.

7. On Septermber 14, 1970, President Park revised the Constitution to allow himself to serve as president for more than two terms. On October 21, this revision was approved by a government-controlled referendum.

8. A popular saying rooted in the fact that the National Assembly has become a rubber stamp. Assemblymen are therefore free to spend their time in other pursuits.

9. A reference to the Yi dynasty tombstones that have been sold to the Japanese for use in the latter's stone gardens.

10. According to a timetable released in the government's third five-year plan, exports are slated to reach US$10 billion by 1980.

11. In the early years of its rule, the Park regime failed completely to devise an agricultural reform policy. American aid grains were used to depress the market price of domestically grown rice, thus forcing peasants off the farms and into the factories.

12. The Park regime initiated a program aimed at substituting imported oil for coal as the nation's primary energy source. Naturally, the domestic coal mining industry suffered a serious decline as a result. With the oil crisis, however, government policy has shifted back to a renewed emphasis upon coal.

13. The Koreans have traditionally burned anthracite briquettes in specially fitted iron burners to heat their homes. With the shift to oil, new burners had to be bought by every household, placing a serious strain on the budgets of most. With the return to coal, the oil burner has had to be put aside.

14. "Waste not even the head of a nail," an aphorism popularized by the government in its drive for thrift and the conservation of scarce materials and resources.

15. In order to attract development capital, President Park has dangled a cheap, skilled and docile work force before foreign investors. In addition to passing laws outlawing labor strikes in foreign enterprises, "tax-free" zones have been set up. Foreign companies participating in such zones are completely exempt from income, property and acquisition taxes for the first five years of their operation, and are fifty percent exempt for the next three years. "Export zones" have also been established "to increase employment and improve technology," all goods produced therein being for export only. Profit transfer rights offered to foreign investors allow hundreds of millions of dollars of untaxed profits to flow out of Korea annually, profits which derive primarily from the low wages paid Korean labor.

16. The "Provisional Special Law Concerning Labor Unions in Foreign Enterprises and the Grievance Arbitration Law," enacted in December, 1969, prohibits strikes or grievance actions by workers.

17. The government's desire to promote the expansion of the heavy and chemical industries has led it to permit foreign enterprises to pollute the environment without restriction.

18. In 1972, Park inaugurated a series of meetings with the North aimed at unification. They have broken down over procedural differences.

19. On November 13, 1971, Chon Tai Il, a worker who tried unsuccessfully to organize Seoul's garment workers, burned himself to death to protest Korean labor's inability to improve its estate.

20. The *Wawoo* Apartment complex, built by the Seoul metropolitan government, collapsed in April, 1970, due to cheap and faulty construction.

21. The Korean government's most recent five-year development plan does contain provisions for increased domestic food production, the enlargement of agricultural income and the improvement of the agricultural environment.

22. In recent years, the government promoted a new strain of rice which could be harvested twice a year. But the strain proved unadaptable to Korean soil, resulting in poor harvests during the early 1970s.

23. The government controls the price of fertilizer, while a farmer must buy into an "agricultural cooperative" before being permitted to purchase any. He is thus required to buy the right to buy.

24. The government has purchased rice from abroad and sold it at a price below that of domestic grain, adding further pressure on the farm population to abandon the countryside and find employment in industry.

25. Since 1968, the Park government has required that on several days each week the population substitute wheat and other grains for the traditional diet of rice. This policy stresses dependence on foreign sources of agricultural products to free the rural populace for employment in the nation's factories.

26. A government-designed program inaugurated in April 1970 to upgrade the rural living standard. To date, the program has been mostly rhetoric because other government policies—of higher priority—work to suppress the rural sector in favor of generating a cheap labor supply.

27. The tiger is the emblem of Korea University, which has been at the center of student resistance since the start of Japanese colonial rule in 1910; its nationalistic student body is drawn mostly from poor, rural areas. The eagle is the emblem of Yonsei University, another center of student resistance; its student body comes mostly from urban areas and tends to be influenced by the tenets of Christianity.

28. The student demonstrations of October 1973 marked a peak of public dissatisfaction with Park's new Constitution. The government responded by closing all schools and universities prematurely and by imposing prolonged vacations.

Excerpts from Kim Chi Ha's Statement before the Military Tribunal which Sentenced him to Death:

The only way to save our people is to bring down the dictatorship of the present government. The students are our only hope . . . I may have violated the emergency decrees of the President (outlawing dissent), but I don't believe that I have violated the National Security Law (prohibiting Communist subversion) . . . I did everything to help the students. I did not have any money, so I helped by talking with them. Demonstrations are only part of the student movement. The discussion and projection of one's ideas are also part . . . Standing up despite one's chains is a form of resistance . . . I wrote the poem *Five Bandits* . . . The corrupt government officials whom I criticized in *Five Bandits* are being punished. This result should rightly be attributed to my literary work. . . .

(Statement cut off by the presiding judge)